WELCOME TO CHETHAM'S LIBRARY

Chetham's Library, which was founded in 1653, is the oldest
surviving public library in Britain. It was established under the
will of Humphrey Chetham, a prosperous Manchester textile
merchant, banker and landowner. Chetham also made provision
for a school for forty poor boys (now a specialist music school
of world renown), and for five chained libraries to be placed in
local churches.

The building that houses Chetham's is even older than the
School and Library. It was built in 1421 to accommodate the
priests of Manchester's Collegiate Church and remains one of

the most complete me‌‌ north
west of England. The r
with the magnificent re
for readers and visito

At the time of the
for independent stud ır
governors, appointe up
a major collection of books and manuscripts the
whole range of available knowledge and would rival the college

---

Medieval buildings with courtyard

libraries of Oxford and Cambridge. Today the Library continues to expand, specialising in the history and topography of Greater Manchester and Lancashire.

Humphrey Chetham's will of 1651 stipulated that the Library should be 'for the use of schollars and others well affected', and instructed the librarian 'to require nothing of any man that cometh into the library'. Chetham's has been in continuous use as a free public library for over 350 years, and the strength and breadth of its collections, coupled with its rich history, ensures that the Library continues to be both a significant centre for study and research and a deservedly popular place to visit.

HUMPHREY CHETHAM

Humphrey Chetham (1580–1653), the most successful gentleman merchant of seventeenth-century Lancashire, was born in Crumpsall, near Manchester. His fortune was made in the cloth trade, mainly in buying and selling fustian, a strong woven fabric made of linen and cotton. He was a shrewd and successful businessman, and in the 1620s began to purchase land and property in the Manchester area.

Chetham's wealth brought him into the public domain, although he was a reluctant official, and in 1631 he was fined for refusing a knighthood. In 1634 he was appointed High Sheriff of the County of Lancashire, but refused a second term on the grounds of infirmity and old age.

Portrait of Humphrey Chetham in 1653

For many years before his death Chetham attempted to make provision for a large charitable scheme. Towards the end of his life he began to pay for the education and maintenance of twenty-two boys from the Manchester region. His concern was to overcome poverty by curing ignorance, and to provide the hope of a livelihood for underprivileged boys. The

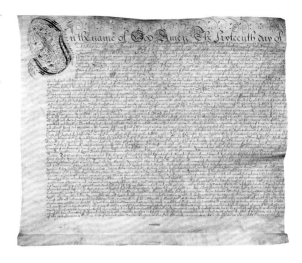

school he founded was known as Chetham's Hospital because it was a place of shelter as well as instruction. Humphrey Chetham died unmarried on 20 September 1653 at the age of 72, and was buried amid much pomp and ceremony at the Collegiate Church of Manchester.

THE CREATION OF THE LIBRARY

The first task facing Humphrey Chetham's governors was to purchase the medieval College House, which, after many years of neglect, was in a poor state. During the Civil War it had been used as a prison and arsenal, and it was remarked that 'the towne swine make there abode bothe in the yards and house'. The restoration was carried out by local craftsmen, and a joiner named Richard Martinscroft was entrusted with the task of fitting and furnishing the Library.

The Library was housed on the first floor in order to avoid rising damp, and the newly acquired books were chained

Bookseller's invoice from Robert Littlebury of London, 17 June 1669

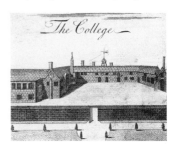

18th-century wall press

Carved oak stool with 'S'-shaped hand-hold

to the bookcases, or presses, in accordance with Chetham's own instructions. Twenty-four carved oak stools with 'S'-shaped hand-holds were provided as portable seats for readers.

In 1655 three of the governors were nominated to choose books, manuscripts and archives for the Library. Almost all of the early acquisitions were bought from a single London bookseller and were packed tightly into old barrels to protect them on the journey. In the first thirty years the Library bought heavily in theology, law, history, medicine and science, and acquired an impressive collection of manuscripts. The aim was to build up as quickly as possible a collection that would meet the needs of the clergy, lawyers and doctors of Manchester and the surrounding towns.

On arrival the books were listed by the Librarian and placed on the presses in size order: large books at the bottom and small

ones at the top. No proper catalogue was published until 1791, and even then the books were listed only by subject and size. To make matters worse, the catalogue was written in Latin. By the mid-eighteenth century the Library's collection had outgrown the original shelves and the presses were increased in height. The practice of chaining was abandoned and, instead, gates were put up to prevent theft. From then on, material was brought to the Reading Room for study, a practice which continues today. The original system of alphabetically labelling each press may still be seen on the oak panels, along with some traces of the early hinges and plates for the chains. This fixed location system is still used today, in conjunction with an electronic catalogue.

HUMPHREY CHETHAM'S PARISH LIBRARIES

Under the terms of Chetham's will the sum of £200 was allocated for the provision of five small libraries, designed to be chained and housed in wooden chests. Chetham wanted them placed in the parish churches of Manchester and Bolton and in the parochial chapelries of Gorton, Turton and Walmsley. The library at Gorton was the first of the five libraries to be completed. It contained fifty-one works and cost nearly £33.

The Library of the Parish Church of St James, 1655

The governors were instructed to purchase 'godly Englishe Bookes ... for the edification of the common people'. As was still common practice at the time the books were shelved with the fore-edge rather than the spine facing outwards to prevent the chains from rubbing against the bindings.

Of the five original libraries only two have survived, those of Gorton and Turton. The Manchester library was dispersed about 1830 and the books ended up at second-hand bookstalls in nearby Shudehill. A number of the books belonging to the Bolton library are to be found in a chained library given by James Lever to Bolton School in 1694. The library intended for Walmsley was never completed.

In 1984 the chained library of Gorton was placed in Chetham's Library on permanent loan and was bought outright with the help of a Lottery grant in 2001.

THE LIBRARY'S COLLECTIONS

Manuscripts and Archives
From illuminated manuscripts made for kings and queens to the minutiae of personal life – diaries, letters, account books – the Library has a wealth of special items and collections. Chetham's holds over forty medieval manuscripts, including the thirteenth-century *Flores Historiarum* of Matthew Paris – a chronicle of English and world history; a fifteenth-century Aulus Gellius, bound for Matthias Corvinus, King of Hungary; and an important compendium of Middle English poetry. Among the modern manuscripts are Horace Walpole's account of money spent on his house at Strawberry Hill, and a seventeenth-century prose and verse miscellany containing letters by Ralegh and Bacon, and

Coronation of Arthur from the *Flores Historiarum* of Matthew Paris (mid-13th to early 14th century, English)

Aulus Gellius, *Noctes Atticae*, manuscript written in Florence *c.* 1472 and bound in red goatskin tooled in gold for Matthias Corvinus, King of Hungary (d. 1490)

Illuminated page from Aulus Gellius' *Noctes Atticae*

Illustration from a 16th-century emblem book

poems by Donne and Jonson. There are four works by the poet Robert Southey, notably his *Letters of Espriella*, in which he offered his view of Manchester: 'a place more destitute of all interest it is impossible to conceive'.

The manuscript and archival collections are mainly concerned with the history of the north west of England. There are extensive collections of title deeds, institutional records and antiquarian papers collected and compiled by local historians. Chetham's has the oldest history of Manchester – Richard Hollingworth's 1656 autograph of *Mancuniensis*; numerous social, economic and political papers, including wages books of early mills, accounts of the poor house and the overseers-of-the-poor; and the first ever census of Manchester, compiled in 1773–74.

Belle Vue

One of the largest institutional collections concerns Belle Vue Zoo and Gardens. Until its closure in the 1970s, Belle Vue was Manchester's principal centre of entertainment and the country's most important provincial zoo. Founded on the eastern side of the city in 1836 by John Jennison (1793–1869), Belle Vue was also famous for hosting numerous other activities: firework displays, brass band contests, ballroom dancing, pop concerts and political meetings. Other attractions included an amusement park, circus and speedway.

Belle Vue Zoo programme

The Belle Vue archive has been assembled by the Library over a period of sixty years and contains thousands of posters, programmes and photographs, as well as the financial and business papers of the owners. These include a notebook recording payments for such diverse items as butter, potatoes, cigars, meat for the animals, and in June 1854, £400 for an unspecified number of lions.

Printed books

There are well over 120,000 printed items, of which over half were published before 1850. Most of the Library's earliest acquisitions were bought second-hand and many of these have an interesting provenance. Ben Jonson's copy of Plato for example, was bought in 1655 for the sum of £3 10 shillings. A 1539 copy of Prosper of Aquitaine, which was bound in white deerskin for Henry VIII, was bought in 1674 for only 8 shillings. Although these rare volumes, ironically, were acquired relatively cheaply, printed books were extremely valuable commodities.

Prosper of Aquitaine, *Opera* (Lyon, 1539), bound in white deerskin tooled in gold with the arms and motto of Henry VIII

The Library was prepared to spend vast sums of money on particularly desirable volumes, paying as much as £20, for example, for an eight-volume Bible. By comparison, the first Chetham's Librarian was paid £10, plus board and lodging, for a year's work.

The first book acquired by the Library, an eleven-volume set of the works of St Augustine for which the Library paid the sum of £7, set the standard for a very large and particularly fine collection of theology. There is a good collection of Bibles, with all four of the great Polyglots represented, as well as Erasmus's New Testament in the original Greek. There are extensive holdings of patristic and reformation theology, church history and liturgy. The Library also has

Map of Lancashire (1577), from Christopher Saxton's *Atlas of the Counties of England and Wales* (London, 1579)

a first edition of Cranmer's *Booke of Common Prayer* (1549), the first single manual of worship in a vernacular language.

Of the secular history books perhaps the most important is a copy of Hartmann Schedel's magnificent *Nuremberg Chronicle* of 1493, complete with a sixteenth-century translation into English in the margin – the only time this work has ever been translated. English history includes all of the major town and county histories, and a large collection of books on heraldry and genealogy. There are extensive holdings of topography and maps, of which Christopher Saxton's atlas of 1579, the first printed atlas of England and Wales, is the best known.

The Library's scientific collections are even more impressive: Aristotle, Euclid, Galileo, Copernicus and Kepler were all acquired at the outset, as were outstanding works of natural history and medicine, notably early editions of Galen and Hippocrates. The Library also showed an interest in the new science, and bought first editions of Robert Hooke's *Micrographia* (1665) and Isaac Newton's *Principia Mathematica*

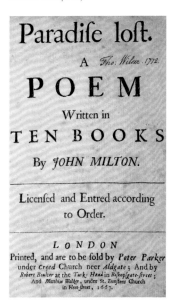

Title-page of *Paradise Lost* (with former owner's inscription)

Portrait of John Milton from the binding of the Foulis brothers' Glasgow edition of *Paradise Lost* (1770)

(1687). The literature collection contains virtually all of the Greek and Latin classics, including the first printing of Homer (1488) and Plutarch's *Lives* (1517), as well as editions published by many of the great printing houses of Europe – Jenson, Aldus, Estienne, Plantin and Elsevir. English literature is strong in drama and poetry, with

many first editions of key works such as Samuel Johnson's *Dictionary of the English Language* (1755) and Milton's *Paradise Lost* (1667).

The scholarly collection of books begun by Humphrey Chetham's governors in the seventeenth century is only a part of the Library's holdings. By the mid-eighteenth century the Library began to acquire large illustrated works and multi-volume periodicals and journals, and a century later the emphasis shifted again. Until the nineteenth century Chetham's had been the only repository for books and printed matter in Manchester, but with the creation of rate-supported public libraries, the governors agreed that the policy of buying books on all subjects could no longer be sustained. Instead the decision was made to specialise in the history and topography of the north west of England. Chetham's now has one of the largest collections of material relating to Manchester and its region, with extensive holdings of prints, maps and photographic slides, and large runs of newspapers, trade directories and periodicals.

The paraphernalia of everyday life
As well as printed books and manuscripts Chetham's has an enormous amount of ephemera, with particularly rich collections of bookplates, postcards, chapbooks, broadsides, ballads, theatre programmes, posters, trade cards and bill heads. Many of these were given to the Library in 1852 by the Shakespearean scholar, James

The Messenger of Mortality: or a Dialogue Between Death and the Lady, hand-coloured broadside from the Halliwell-Phillips collection

The Old House of Corrections, watercolour by Thomas Barritt, 1819, from the Earl of Ellesmere's Manchester Scrapbook

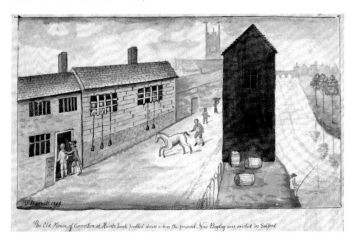

The Old House of Correction at Hunts bank pulled down when the present New Bayley was erected in Salford

Orchard Halliwell-Phillipps. His collection of over 3,100 items contains many unique works: fragments of medieval manuscripts; sixteenth-century black-letter ballads; political, social and commercial broadsides; and songs and music dating from 1680 to 1750.

There are many albums and scrapbooks of local material, including rare specimens of Manchester printing. One album, for example, known as the 'Cambrics Scrapbook', contains over 250 broadsheets, ranging from light-hearted entertainment handbills to notices of serious political issues, mostly dating from the end of the eighteenth century. Another work, the 'Manchester Scrapbook', was compiled by the Earl of Elles-mere and given to the Library in 1838. This work contains almost 400 items, including pen-and-ink sketches of local characters, scenes and customs.

Peter Manchester, hand-coloured engraving by N. Orme, from the Earl of Ellesmere's Manchester Scrapbook

PETER MANCHESTER.

A CABINET OF CURIOSITIES

For much of its history Chetham's was home to a bizarre collection of curiosities, including a woman's skeleton, an alligator's skin, a young swordfish, a flying stag, the tail of a rattle snake, the shells of an ostrich egg, two coconuts, a large calabash, a branch of white coral, a lodestone, a tortoise shell, a hummingbird and an enormous stone taken out of a woman's bladder. The collection featured in some of Manchester's first guidebooks and made the Library something of a tourist attraction. The writer Celia Fiennes visited Manchester in 1698 and claimed: 'There I saw the skinn of a rattle snake 6 foote long with many other Curiositys, their anatomy of a man wired together, and the jaw of a sherke ...'.

Little Major, the tollkeeper at the New Bailey Bridge, from the Earl of Ellesmere's Manchester Scrapbook

In the nineteenth century some couples incorporated a visit to the Library's museum as part of their wedding arrangements. A local ballad, *Johnny Green's Wedding and Description of Manchester College*, recounts the practice by which Oldham couples would walk into Manchester on Easter Monday in large numbers to marry at the Collegiate Church. Afterwards, the wedding party, most of whom were the worse for wear from drink, would tour the College to marvel at the curiosities on display.

The Learned Pig, detail from a Manchester broadside of 1787

The Learned P I G, from London.

MARX AND ENGELS

The great radical philosopher and father of communism, Karl Marx, spent time studying at Chetham's Library during the middle years of the nineteenth century. His friend and close collaborator, Friedrich Engels, was employed from 1842 to 1869 at his father's Salford cotton manufacturing firm, working his way up from office clerk to joint proprietor. Although he disliked the work it enabled him to offer financial support to Marx and his family, who had very little income. Marx was a frequent visitor to Manchester and was able to observe at first hand the appalling living conditions of the working classes in the tightly packed streets and alleyways of the city.

Marx's first visit to Chetham's took place in the summer of 1845. He later told his publisher that the journey had been taken in order to undertake research for his book on political economy. Evidently the Library made a strong impression on the two men. Writing to Marx in 1870 Engels commented:

> During the last few days I have again spent a good deal of time sitting at the four-sided desk in the alcove where we sat together twenty-four years ago. I am very fond of the place. The stained

The alcove where Karl Marx and Friedrich Engels worked together in the summer of 1845

16th- and 17th-century pocket books

glass window ensures that the weather is always fine there. Old Jones, the Librarian, is still alive but he is very old and no longer active. I have not seen him on this occasion.

The desk where Marx and Engels sat together remains in the Reading Room alcove, and the books they consulted in 1845 are still held by the Library.

CHETHAM'S MEDIEVAL ROOTS

Chetham's is built on a sandstone outcrop at the confluence of the Rivers Irwell and Irk, a site of strategic importance which has been occupied since Roman times. The present building dates from the second quarter of the fifteenth century. In 1421 Thomas de la Warre, Lord of Manchester and rector of the parish church, obtained a licence from Henry V to re-found the church as a collegiate body, with a warden, eight fellows, four clerks and six lay choristers.

Medieval doorway leading off the south cloister

De la Warre gave up his own manor house and land for the impressive new building, which was built of local sandstone, quarried in Collyhurst and brought to the site by river barge. The generous accommodation included a large hall, the warden's own lodgings and a set of rooms for each of the fellows. In addition, the complex had its own bakehouse, brewery and stables, as well as ample domestic facilities and guest rooms. Other than the church it was the largest building in the medieval town of Manchester.

The survival of such a complete medieval domestic building is rare in itself, and its troubled history makes that survival all the more surprising.

In 1547 the College was dissolved and the Stanley family acquired the property as a town residence. The College was re-founded, closed down and re-opened, but gradually fell into a state of disrepair until its triumphant resurrection as the vessel for Humphrey Chetham's glorious legacy.

A great deal of what Chetham's governors accomplished in putting right the years of neglect remains visible in the building today. The rooms, passageways and courtyards have much to reveal to us of the institution's remarkable history.

Gatehouse

Grant by letters patent of Edward VI of the College House of Manchester and other property to Edward third Earl of Derby and his heirs, 9 July 1549

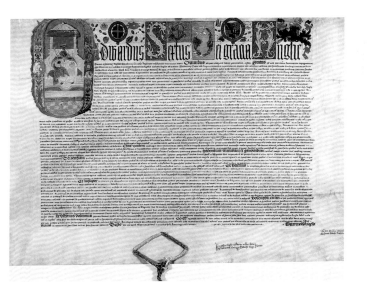

Cloister Court

The three-sided cloisters are ranged around a small, cobbled courtyard, and the stone doorways which originally led to the fellows' rooms can still be seen. Each of the ground floor rooms had a fireplace and was of a generous size. Unusually, the cloister has two storeys, and the upper walk once gave access to the fellows' bed chambers. The courtyard has become known as the Fox Court, owing to an optical illusion: on looking through one of the three openings at the top of the old stone well, the light of the other two is reflected in the water, giving the impression of the eyes of an animal.

West wing of the medieval double-storeyed cloisters

Audit Room

This is one of the most richly appointed in the building and was one of the rooms allocated to the warden of the medieval college. The most notable decorative feature is the timber ceiling, divided into nine panels by moulded ribs decorated with bosses. The most grotesque is a Mouth of Hell, with a sinner ensnared in its jaws. The bosses date from the second half of the fifteenth century, and there are some similarities with the panels in the roof of the choir of Manchester Cathedral.

Detail of the Audit Room medieval roof timber, depicting a Hell Mouth

Chetham's governors remodelled the room in the seventeenth century and provided it with its elaborate plasterwork, oak panelling and doors. The furniture includes a three-legged chair

Audit Room

said to have belonged to Humphrey Chetham, and some carved panel-back chairs typical of the north country. There are also eighteenth-century items: a set of twelve ladder-back mahogany chairs; a handsome walnut settee with cabriole legs resting on ball-and-claw feet; and a one-fingered lantern clock, still in good, albeit noisy, working order.

The large oak refectory table bears a strange mark in one corner, said, according to legend, to represent the devil's hoofprint. In 1595 the wardenship of the College passed to John Dee, a member of the court of Queen Elizabeth and a learned scientist, astronomer, mathematician and philosopher. His reputation as an alchemist and student of the occult was well established and his arcane endeavours are supposed to have resulted in the appearance of the devil, who materialised over the table and left behind the mark of his hoof.

Reading Room
The magnificent Reading Room contains some of the most beautiful furniture in the building, with its Cromwellian gate-legged table, one of the largest of its type in existence, and twenty-four leather-backed chairs. Above the fireplace is an elaborate heraldic and emblematic display commemorating

Reading Room

Chetham and his foundation. His coat of arms is in the centre, flanked by obelisks resting on books and supporting torches symbolic of learning. To the left is a cock and to the right a pelican in piety – a traditional symbol of Christ's sacrifice.

Baronial Hall
The Hall is a wonderfully preserved example of the timber-roofed halls found in the north west of England, and is comparable in size with Ordsall Hall, Salford, and Rufford Hall, Lancashire. The magnificent roof once accommodated a louvre opening to let out the smoke from a central hearth. Some time during the sixteenth or seventeenth centuries this was replaced by a simple fireplace with a shallow lintel, which was in turn replaced in the nineteenth century by the large inglenook fireplace still there today. The current stone flagged floor was laid in the mid-seventeenth century as part of the alterations made by the governors of Chetham's. The hall retains the beautiful oak screen of three equal sections. At the top of the Hall an impressive oak canopy projects over a dais, where the warden and fellows would have dined at high table.

Baronial Hall

Association Room

Until recently this was the kitchen of the College and School. Open from floor to roof, and lit by two lines of windows facing the courtyard, it contains the remains of two fireplaces. The larger, in the north wall, has a fine joggled lintel with a relieving arch, above which are various cooking implements.

Underneath the Association Room there is an extensive network of cellars, which at one time gave access to the River Irk – an important transport link and source of fish in the early days of the building's history. Early drawings of this aspect of the College building show steps leading down to the riverbank and a boathouse. One of these cellars was known as the 'snake pit', probably due to the presence of eels that would emerge from the River Irk to seek the milk which was stored there.

LOOKING FORWARD

Chetham's Library remains an independent charity and continues to be administered by twenty-four governors. In recent years, thanks largely to Heritage Lottery funding, we have been able to conserve many of the most fragile items in the collection, repairing and restoring many thousands of historic bindings. We have also created an online catalogue for many of the printed books, enabling our holdings to be available to anyone in the world with the use of a computer. In the course of this cataloguing work we have unearthed many treasures, not least over 200 Hogarth engravings, and a collection of fifteenth-century letters written by members of a gentry family, the largest to have been discovered since the nineteenth century. This work continues. As a major rare book repository and as a nationally significant centre for the study of history, it is essential that the Library continues to develop its collections relating to the north west of England, and to fill gaps in its older historic collections. Material is still being added, by purchase and by donation. Recently, for example, we have acquired a set of thirty-two nineteenth-century diaries compiled by members of a prominent Manchester family, together with a large collection of business papers from one of Manchester's earliest textile mills.

Chetham's provides a unique testimony to a Manchester long since vanished. For over 350 years the Library has been a place of bibliographic pilgrimage. In few other places can the growth of a historic library be studied in such depth, from such a wealth of materials, in surroundings so appropriate.

Priests' Wing

Manchester Ballad Seller, hand-coloured engraving, from the Earl of Ellesmere's Manchester Scrapbook

Chetham's Library is open to visitors and readers Monday to Friday 9am–12.30pm and 1.30–4.30pm.

Readers are required to make an appointment. Please note that Chetham's is a working building and there are likely to be times when some of the rooms are not available for viewing. The Library or parts of it may have to close from time to time for special circumstances without prior notice.

Chetham's School and Library
Long Millgate, Manchester M3 1SB

Tel 0161 834 7961
Fax 0161 839 5797
Email librarian@chethams.org.uk
Website www.chethams.org.uk

© Scala Publishers Ltd, 2008
© Text Chetham's Library
© Photography Becky Lingard and Fergus Wilde

First published in 2008 by
Scala Publishers Ltd
Northburgh House
10 Northburgh Street
London EC1V 0AT, UK
www.scalapublishers.com

ISBN 978 1 85759 556 7

Edited by Sandra Pisano
Designed by Andrew Shoolbred
Printed in Singapore

10 9 8 7 6 5 4 3 2 1

FRONT COVER: Mary Chapel Wing

BACK COVER: Courtyard showing Hyde's Cross

FRONT AND BACK FLAPS: Hand-coloured wood block from *Cologne Chronicle* (1499)

INSIDE FRONT COVER AND FLAP: *The South West Prospect of Manchester and Salford*, Robert Whitworth, hand-coloured engraving, 1734

INSIDE BACK COVER AND FLAP: *Manchester Cross and Market Place*, E. Goodwin, 1807, from the Earl of Ellesmere's Manchester Scrapbook